THE POWER OF L....

A PRACTICAL INTRODUCTION

OLIVER LUCAS JR

TABLE OF CONTENTS

Chapter 1

Chapter 2

Chapter 3

Chapter 4

Chapter 5

Chapter 6

Chapter 7

Chapter 8

Chapter 9

Chapter 10

Preface

The Power of LLMs: A Practical Introduction

In the tapestry of technological advancement, few innovations have captured the imagination quite like Large Language Models (LLMs). These powerful AI systems are reshaping industries, transforming the way we interact with information, and pushing the boundaries of human creativity.

This book is your guide to understanding and harnessing the power of LLMs. We'll delve into the fundamental concepts, explore their diverse applications, and discuss the ethical implications of their use. Whether you're a seasoned AI practitioner or a curious beginner, this book will equip you with the knowledge to navigate the exciting world of LLMs.

Within these pages, you'll discover:

The Evolution of AI: A historical perspective on the development of AI, from its early beginnings to the rise of LLMs.

The Core Concepts of LLMs: A deep dive into the underlying principles and techniques that power LLMs.

Real-world Applications: Exploring the practical use cases of LLMs across various industries, from healthcare to finance.

Ethical Considerations: Discussing the ethical implications of LLMs and the importance of responsible AI development.

The Future of LLMs: A glimpse into the future, exploring potential advancements and their impact on society.

As you embark on this journey, remember that LLMs are not just tools, but powerful instruments for innovation and positive change. By understanding their capabilities and limitations, we can harness their potential to create a better future for all.

Chapter 1

Introduction to AI and Machine Learning

1.1 A Brief History of AI

The concept of artificial intelligence (AI) has captivated human imagination for centuries, dating back to ancient myths and legends of artificial beings. However, the formal study of AI began in the mid-20th century, fueled by advances in computer science and mathematics.

Early Beginnings (1950s-1970s)

The Dartmouth Conference (1956): This landmark event marked the birth of AI as a formal field of study. Pioneering computer scientists like John McCarthy, Marvin Minsky, and Allen Newell gathered to discuss and explore the potential of creating intelligent machines.

Early AI Programs: Researchers developed programs that could solve mathematical problems, play games like checkers and chess, and even engage in simple conversations. However, these early systems were limited by computational constraints and the lack of sophisticated algorithms.

AI Winter (1970s): The initial wave of AI enthusiasm waned as researchers encountered challenges in scaling up AI systems and achieving human-level intelligence. This period, known as the "AI winter," saw a decline in funding and interest in the field.

The Rise of Expert Systems (1980s-1990s)

Knowledge-Based Systems: AI researchers focused on developing expert systems, which could mimic the decision-making abilities of human experts in specific domains. These systems were used in various fields, including medicine, finance, and engineering.

Machine Learning: The foundations of machine learning were laid during this period. Algorithms like decision trees and neural networks were developed to enable computers to learn from data and make predictions.

The AI Renaissance (2000s-Present)

Big Data and Computational Power: The availability of massive amounts of data and the increasing power of computers fueled a resurgence of AI research.

Deep Learning Revolution: Deep learning, a subset of machine learning, has revolutionized AI. Deep neural networks with multiple layers can learn complex patterns and representations from data, leading to breakthroughs in image recognition, natural language processing, and speech recognition.

AI in Everyday Life: AI has become an integral part of our daily lives, powering applications like voice assistants, recommendation systems, and self-driving cars.

Ethical Considerations: As AI becomes more powerful, it raises important ethical questions regarding bias, transparency, and the potential impact on society.

Today, AI continues to evolve rapidly, with new techniques and applications emerging constantly. While challenges remain, the future of AI holds immense promise for transforming various industries and improving human lives.

1.2 Fundamental Concepts of Machine Learning

Machine learning is a subset of artificial intelligence that empowers computers to learn from data without explicit programming.[1] Here are some fundamental concepts:

Types of Machine Learning

Supervised Learning:

Regression: Predicting a continuous numerical value (e.g., house prices, stock prices).

Classification: Categorizing data into discrete classes (e.g., spam or not spam, cat or dog).

Unsupervised Learning:

Clustering: Grouping similar data points together (e.g., customer segmentation).

Dimensionality Reduction: Reducing the number of features[2] in a dataset (e.g., PCA).

Reinforcement Learning:

Learning through trial and error, where an agent interacts with an environment and receives rewards or penalties for its actions.

Key Concepts

Model: A mathematical representation of a real-world phenomenon.

Features: The input variables used to train a model.

Target Variable: The output variable we want to predict.

Training Data: The dataset used to train a model.

Test Data: A separate dataset used to evaluate the model's performance.

Model Training: The process of adjusting the model's parameters to minimize the error between its predictions and the actual values in the training data.

Model Evaluation: Assessing the model's performance on unseen data using metrics like accuracy, precision, recall, and F1-score.

Overfitting: When a model becomes too complex and fits the training data too closely, leading to poor performance on new data.

Underfitting: When a model is too simple and fails to capture the underlying patterns in the data.

Bias-Variance Trade-off: A balance between model complexity and its ability to generalize to new data.

Common Algorithms

Linear Regression: Models the relationship between a dependent variable and one or more independent variables using a linear equation.

Logistic Regression:[3] Used for classification tasks, predicting the probability of a binary outcome.

Decision Trees: Tree-like models that make decisions based on a series of rules.

Random Forest: An ensemble method that combines multiple decision trees to improve accuracy.

Support Vector Machines (SVM): Finds the optimal hyperplane to separate data points into different classes.

Naive Bayes: A probabilistic classifier based on Bayes' theorem.

K-Nearest Neighbors (KNN): Classifies data points based on the majority class of their nearest neighbors.

Neural Networks: Inspired by the human brain, neural networks consist of interconnected nodes that process information.

Deep Learning: A subset of machine learning that uses deep neural networks with multiple layers to learn complex patterns.

By understanding these fundamental concepts, you can effectively apply machine learning techniques to solve a wide range of real-world problems.

1.3 The Evolution of AI: From Narrow to General Intelligence

Artificial Intelligence (AI) has evolved significantly over the past few decades, transitioning from simple, task-specific systems to more sophisticated and versatile capabilities. This evolution can be broadly categorized into two main types:

1. Narrow AI (Weak AI)

Definition: Narrow AI, also known as Weak AI, is designed to perform specific tasks with a high degree of accuracy.

Examples:

Image recognition: Identifying objects in images or videos.

Speech recognition: Transcribing spoken language into text.

Natural language processing: Understanding and responding to human language.

Recommendation systems: Suggesting products or content based on user preferences.

Game-playing AI: Mastering complex games like chess and Go.

2. General AI (Strong AI)

Definition: General AI, or Strong AI, refers to AI systems that possess human-level intelligence and can understand, learn, and apply knowledge across a wide range of tasks.

Current Status: While significant progress has been made in AI, achieving true General AI remains a distant goal.

Potential Applications:

Scientific research: Accelerating discoveries and solving complex problems.

Healthcare: Developing advanced medical treatments and personalized medicine.

Education: Tailoring education to individual needs and learning styles.

Climate change: Modeling complex climate systems and developing innovative solutions.

The Path Towards General AI

While Narrow AI has made remarkable strides, the path to General AI is still fraught with challenges. Key areas of research and development include:

Cognitive Abilities: Developing AI systems capable of reasoning, problem-solving, and decision-making.

Common Sense: Endowing AI with the ability to understand and apply real-world knowledge.

Learning and Adaptation: Enabling AI to learn from experience and adapt to new situations.

Social Intelligence: Developing AI systems that can understand and respond to human emotions and social cues.

As AI continues to evolve, it is essential to consider the ethical implications and societal impact of these advancements. By addressing challenges and harnessing the potential of AI, we can shape a future where humans and machines work together to solve global problems and improve the quality of life for all.

Chapter 2

Understanding Language Models

2.1 What is a Language Model?

A language model is a type of artificial intelligence that is designed to understand and generate human language.[1]It's trained on vast amounts of text data, allowing it to recognize patterns, predict the next word in a sentence, and generate human-quality text.

How does it work? A language model works by assigning probabilities to sequences of words. For example, given the words "I like to eat", the model can predict the most likely next word, such as "pizza". The model learns these probabilities from the vast amount of text data it's trained on.

Applications of Language Models Language models have a wide range of applications, including:

Natural language processing: Understanding and responding to human language.

Machine translation: Translating text from one language to another.

Text summarization: Condensing long texts into shorter summaries.

Text generation: Creating different kinds of creative content, such as poems, scripts, or code.

Chatbots and virtual assistants: Providing information and completing tasks through conversation.

A popular example of a language model is GPT-3. It's capable of generating human-quality text, translating languages, writing different kinds of creative content, and answering your questions in an informative way.

2.2 Traditional Language Models

Traditional language models, also known as statistical language models, are probabilistic models that predict the likelihood of a sequence of words. These models have been fundamental in natural language processing (NLP) for many years.

Key Types of Traditional Language Models

N-gram Models:

These models predict the probability of a word based on the preceding N-1 words.

For example, a trigram model (N=3) would predict the third word based on the first two.

While simple, N-gram models can be effective for tasks like language modeling and speech recognition.

Hidden Markov Models (HMMs):

HMMs model sequences of observations, such as words in a sentence, by assuming a hidden state that generates the observations.

They're commonly used for tasks like part-of-speech tagging and speech recognition.

Neural Network-based Models:

While neural networks are often associated with modern language models, early neural network models were used for language tasks.

Recurrent Neural Networks (RNNs) and their variants, like Long Short-Term Memory (LSTM) networks, have been particularly influential in language modeling.

These models can capture long-range dependencies in text, making them more powerful than traditional statistical models.

Limitations of Traditional Language Models

While traditional language models have been valuable tools, they have limitations:

Data Sparsity: They often struggle with rare words and phrases, as they rely on statistical frequencies.

Lack of Contextual Understanding: They may not fully capture the semantic and syntactic nuances of language.

Computational Complexity: Some models, especially neural network-based ones, can be computationally expensive to train and use.

The Rise of Large Language Models (LLMs)

In recent years, the advent of large language models (LLMs) has revolutionized the field of NLP. LLMs, powered by deep learning techniques, can handle complex language tasks with unprecedented accuracy and fluency. They overcome many of the limitations of traditional models by leveraging massive amounts of data and advanced neural network architectures.

While traditional language models have laid the foundation for modern NLP, LLMs have significantly advanced the state-of-the-art and continue to push the boundaries of what's possible in AI.

2.3 The Rise of Neural Networks

Neural networks, inspired by the human brain, have emerged as a powerful tool in the field of artificial intelligence.[1]They have revolutionized various domains, from image and speech recognition to natural language processing.

Early Neural Networks

Perceptron: One of the earliest neural network models, the perceptron can learn to classify input data into categories.

Multilayer Perceptron (MLP): MLPs introduced hidden layers, allowing them to learn more complex patterns.

Backpropagation: A crucial algorithm for training neural networks, backpropagation enables the network to adjust its weights and biases to minimize error.

The Deep Learning Revolution

Deep Neural Networks: With the advent of powerful computing hardware and large datasets, deep neural networks, which have multiple layers, have become increasingly popular.

Convolutional Neural Networks (CNNs): CNNs are particularly well-suited for image and video analysis.[7] They use convolutional layers to extract features from input data.

Recurrent Neural Networks (RNNs): RNNs are designed to process sequential data, such as text and time series data.[9] They have memory cells that can store information about past inputs.

Long Short-Term Memory (LSTM) Networks: A type of RNN that can learn long-term dependencies, making them suitable for tasks like machine translation and text generation.

Transformer Networks: A more recent architecture that has revolutionized natural language processing.[12]Transformers use attention mechanisms to weigh the importance of different parts of the input sequence.

Key Advantages of Neural Networks

Feature Learning: Neural networks can automatically learn relevant features from data, reducing the need for manual feature engineering.

Adaptability: They can adapt to new data and improve their performance over time.

Powerful Representation Learning: Neural networks can capture complex patterns and relationships in data.

End-to-End Learning: They can learn directly from raw input data to output predictions, eliminating the need for multiple stages of processing.

Neural networks have the potential to solve complex problems and drive innovation in various fields.[18] As research continues to advance, we can expect even more powerful and versatile neural network architectures to emerge.

Chapter 3

The Emergence of Large Language Models (LLMs)

3.1 The Transformer Architecture

The Transformer architecture, introduced in the paper "Attention Is All You Need," has revolutionized the field of natural language processing (NLP). Unlike traditional sequence-to-sequence models like RNNs and LSTMs, Transformers rely solely on an attention mechanism to weigh the importance of different parts of the input sequence.

Key Components of a Transformer:

Encoder:

Input Embedding: Converts input tokens (words or subwords) into numerical representations.

Positional Encoding: Adds positional information to the input embeddings, as Transformers don't have a sequential processing mechanism like RNNs.

Encoder-Decoder Attention Layer: This layer allows the model to attend to relevant parts of the input sequence when processing each token.

Feed-Forward Neural Network: Applies transformations to each position independently.

Decoder:

Decoder-Decoder Self-Attention: Similar to the encoder-decoder attention, but it allows the decoder to attend to its own generated output.

Encoder-Decoder Attention: Allows the decoder to attend to the relevant parts of the encoded input sequence.

Feed-Forward Neural Network: Applies transformations to each position independently.

Output Layer: Generates the final output sequence, token by token.

Why Transformers are Powerful:

Parallel Processing: Transformers can process input sequences in parallel, making them more efficient than sequential models like RNNs.

Long-Range Dependencies: The attention mechanism allows Transformers to capture long-range dependencies between words, which is crucial for tasks like machine translation and text summarization.

Flexibility: Transformers can be applied to a wide range of NLP tasks, such as text classification, question answering, and text generation.

Impact of Transformers

The Transformer architecture has led to significant advancementsin NLP, enabling state-of-the-art performance on various tasks. Some notable examples include:

GPT-3: A powerful language model capable of generating human-quality text.

BERT: A bidirectional language model for understanding the context of words in a sentence.

T5: A text-to-text transfer transformer, which can be fine-tuned for various NLP tasks.

By understanding the fundamental principles of the Transformer architecture, you can appreciate the power and versatility of this groundbreaking model.

3.2 Training LLMs: Data, Hardware, and Algorithms

Training large language models (LLMs) is a complex and resource-intensive process that requires a careful consideration of data, hardware, and algorithms.

Data

Quantity and Quality: LLMs require massive amounts of high-quality text data to learn language patterns and generate coherent text. This data often comes from books, articles, code repositories, and other sources.

Data Cleaning and Preprocessing: The data needs to be cleaned, filtered, and preprocessed to remove noise, inconsistencies, and biases. This includes tasks like tokenization, normalization, and removing irrelevant or harmful content.

Data Augmentation: Techniques like back-translation, text generation, and data synthesis can be used to artificially increase the size and diversity of the training dataset.

Hardware

GPUs: Graphics Processing Units (GPUs) are essential for accelerating the training process. They are designed to handle parallel computations, which is ideal for the matrix operations involved in neural networks.

TPUs: Tensor Processing Units (TPUs) are specialized hardware accelerators designed specifically for machine learning tasks, including LLM training. They offer significant performance gains over GPUs for certain types of workloads.

Distributed Training: To handle the massive computational demands of LLM training, distributed training frameworks are used to distribute the workload across multiple machines, each with multiple GPUs or TPUs.

Algorithms

Transformer Architecture: The Transformer architecture, with its attention mechanism, has become the foundation for many state-of-the-art LLMs. It enables the model to weigh the importance of different parts of the input sequence.

Optimization Algorithms: Algorithms like Adam and RMSprop are used to optimize the model's parameters during training.

Hyperparameter Tuning: The performance of an LLM can be significantly impacted by hyperparameters such as learning rate, batch size, and number of layers. Careful tuning is crucial.

Regularization Techniques: Techniques like dropout and L1/L2 regularization are used to prevent overfitting and improve generalization.

Challenges and Considerations

Computational Cost: Training large language models is extremely expensive, both in terms of hardware and energy consumption.

Data Quality and Bias: The quality and diversity of the training data can significantly impact the model's performance and potential biases.

Ethical Implications: LLMs can perpetuate biases present in the training data, and it's important to consider the ethical implications of their use.

By carefully considering these factors, researchers and engineers can train powerful LLMs that can revolutionize various fields, from natural language processing to healthcare and beyond.

3.3 Key Challenges and Limitations of LLMs

While Large Language Models (LLMs) have made significant strides in recent years, they still face several key challenges and limitations:

1. Factual Accuracy:

LLMs can sometimes generate incorrect or misleading information, especially when presented with prompts that require factual knowledge.

They may hallucinate facts or invent information, leading to errors and inaccuracies.

2. Bias and Fairness:

LLMs can perpetuate biases present in their training data, leading to unfair and discriminatory outputs.

Addressing bias requires careful curation of training data and the development of techniques to mitigate bias during training.

3. Lack of Common Sense and Reasoning:

LLMs often struggle with tasks that require common sense reasoning, such as understanding analogies, metaphors, or real-world situations.

They may generate plausible-sounding but nonsensical or contradictory responses.

4. Overreliance on Training Data:

LLMs are highly dependent on the quality and quantity of their training data.

If the training data is limited or biased, the model's performance may be compromised.

5. Computational Cost:

Training and deploying LLMs is computationally expensive, requiring significant hardware resources and energy consumption.

This limits accessibility and scalability, especially for smaller organizations.

6. Ethical Concerns:

The potential misuse of LLMs, such as generating harmful content or spreading misinformation, raises ethical concerns.

Responsible development and deployment of LLMs is crucial to mitigate these risks.

Addressing these challenges requires ongoing research and development, as well as a commitment to ethical AI practices. By carefully considering the limitations and potential pitfalls of LLMs, we can harness their power while minimizing their negative impacts.

Chapter 4

Capabilities of LLMs

4.1 Text Generation and Summarization

Large Language Models (LLMs) have revolutionized the field of natural language processing, enabling powerful text generation and summarization capabilities.

Text Generation

Text generation involves creating new text, such as articles, poems, scripts, or code. LLMs can generate text in various styles and tones, making them versatile tools for creative writing, content creation, and more.

Key Techniques:

Autoregressive Models: These models generate text token by token, conditioning each prediction on the previously generated tokens.

Non-autoregressive Models: These models generate text in parallel, which can be more efficient for longer sequences.

Applications:

Content Creation: Generating news articles, product descriptions, or social media posts.

Creative Writing: Assisting writers in brainstorming ideas, drafting outlines, or generating creative text formats like poems or scripts.

Code Generation: Autocompleting code, suggesting improvements, or even generating entire code functions.

Text Summarization

Text summarization involves condensing long documents into shorter versions while preserving the key information. LLMs can generate concise and informative summaries.

Key Techniques:

Extractive Summarization: Identifies and extracts the most important sentences from the original text.

Abstractive Summarization: Generates new text that captures the main ideas of the original text.

Applications:

Document Summarization: Summarizing research papers, news articles, or legal documents.

Meeting Summarization: Generating summaries of meetings or lectures.

Customer Reviews Summarization: Condensing customer feedback into key themes and sentiments.

Challenges and Future Directions: While LLMs have made significant strides, there are still challenges to overcome:

Factual Accuracy: Ensuring that generated text is accurate and reliable.

Bias and Fairness: Mitigating biases in training data and model outputs.

Controllability: Developing techniques to control the style, tone, and content of generated text.

Evaluation Metrics: Creating robust metrics to evaluate the quality of generated text and summaries.

As research progresses, we can expect further advancements in text generation and summarization, leading to even more powerful and creative applications.

4.2 Translation and Language Understanding

Large Language Models (LLMs) have significantly advanced the field of machine translation and language understanding.

Machine Translation

Machine translation involves automatically translating text from one language to another. LLMs have made significant strides in improving the quality and fluency of machine translations.

Key Techniques:

Sequence-to-Sequence Models: These models encode the source language sentence into a latent representation and then decode it into the target language.

Transformer-Based Models: Transformers have revolutionized machine translation by enabling more efficient and accurate translations.

Applications:

Language Barriers: Breaking down language barriers and facilitating global communication.

Content Localization: Adapting content to different languages and cultures.

Document Translation: Translating legal, medical, and technical documents.

Language Understanding

Language understanding involves the ability of machines to comprehend and interpret human language. LLMs can understand the nuances of language, including context, sentiment, and intent.

Key Techniques:

Sentiment Analysis: Identifying the sentiment expressed in a text (positive, negative, or neutral).

Text Classification: Categorizing text into predefined categories (e.g., news, sports, politics).

Question Answering: Answering questions based on a given text.

Text Summarization: Condensing long texts into shorter summaries.

Applications:

Chatbots and Virtual Assistants: Enabling natural language interactions with machines.

Information Retrieval: Improving search engine results by understanding the intent behind queries.

Content Moderation: Identifying and filtering harmful or inappropriate content.

Challenges and Future Directions: While LLMs have made significant progress, there are still challenges to overcome:

Language Diversity: Handling low-resource languages and dialects.

Cultural Nuances: Capturing cultural nuances and idiomatic expressions.

Contextual Understanding: Understanding the context of a sentence or paragraph.

Ethical Considerations: Addressing biases and ensuring fairness in language models.

As research continues to advance, we can expect even more sophisticated language models that can bridge language barriers and facilitate human-computer interaction.

4.3 Code Generation and Reasoning

Large Language Models (LLMs) have demonstrated remarkable capabilities in code generation and reasoning. By training on vast amounts of code, LLMs can generate code snippets, complete code functions, and even debug existing code.

Code Generation

LLMs can generate code in various programming languages, making it a valuable tool for developers.

Key Techniques:

Sequence-to-Sequence Models: These models can generate code one token at a time, conditioned on the previous tokens.

Transformer-Based Models: Transformers are particularly well-suited for code generation due to their ability to capture long-range dependencies.

Applications:

Code Completion: Autocompleting code snippets based on context.

Code Generation from Natural Language: Generating code from natural language descriptions.

Code Refactoring: Suggesting improvements to existing code.

Test Case Generation: Generating test cases to ensure code quality.

Code Reasoning

LLMs can reason about code, analyze its correctness, and identify potential errors.

Key Techniques:

Static Code Analysis: Analyzing code without executing it to find potential issues.

Dynamic Code Analysis: Executing code to identify runtime errors and performance bottlenecks.

Program Synthesis: Generating code from formal specifications.

Applications:

Code Debugging: Identifying and fixing errors in code.

Code Optimization: Improving code performance and efficiency.

Code Verification: Verifying the correctness of code.

Challenges and Future Directions: While LLMs have shown promise in code generation and reasoning, there are still challenges to overcome:

Code Quality: Ensuring the generated code is efficient, reliable, and adheres to best practices.

Security Vulnerabilities: Mitigating the risk of generating code with security vulnerabilities.

Domain-Specific Knowledge: Adapting LLMs to specific programming languages and domains.

Ethical Considerations: Addressing the potential misuse of code generation tools.

As research progresses, we can expect LLMs to become even more powerful tools for software development, enabling developers to write better code faster.

Chapter 5

Applications of LLMs

5.1 LLMs in Customer Service: A New Era of Customer Experience

Large Language Models (LLMs) are revolutionizing the way businesses interact with their customers. By integrating LLMs into customer service operations, companies can significantly improve efficiency, customer satisfaction, and overall business outcomes.

Key Applications of LLMs in Customer Service:

Intelligent Chatbots:

24/7 Support: LLMs enable chatbots to provide round-the-clock support, answering common queries and resolving simple issues.

Personalized Interactions: By analyzing customer data, LLMs can tailor responses to individual needs and preferences.

Efficient Problem Solving: LLMs can quickly identify and address customer issues, reducing resolution time.

Enhanced Customer Support:

Knowledge Base Search: LLMs can efficiently search through vast knowledge bases to find accurate and relevant information.

Agent Assistance: LLMs can provide real-time suggestions and guidance to human agents, improving their efficiency and accuracy.

Sentiment Analysis: LLMs can analyze customer sentiment to identify potential issues and proactively address them.

Proactive Customer Engagement:

Personalized Recommendations: LLMs can analyze customer behavior and preferences to offer personalized product recommendations.

Predictive Support: By analyzing historical data, LLMs can anticipate potential customer issues and proactively provide solutions.

Benefits of Using LLMs in Customer Service:

Improved Customer Satisfaction: LLMs can provide faster, more accurate, and more personalized support.

Increased Efficiency: Automation of routine tasks frees up human agents to focus on complex issues.

Reduced Costs: LLMs can help reduce operational costs by automating tasks and reducing the need for human intervention.

Enhanced Brand Reputation: Positive customer experiences drive brand loyalty and advocacy.

While LLMs offer significant potential, it's important to consider ethical implications and potential biases. By carefully training and monitoring LLMs, businesses can ensure that they are used responsibly and ethically.

As LLM technology continues to evolve, we can expect even more innovative applications in customer service, further transforming the way businesses interact with their customers.

5.2 LLMs in Education: A New Era of Personalized Learning

Large Language Models (LLMs) are poised to revolutionize the education sector. By leveraging their ability to process and generate human-quality text, LLMs can offer a wide range of benefits to both students and educators.

Personalized Learning

Tailored Curriculum: LLMs can analyze individual student performance and learning styles to create customized learning paths.

Adaptive Learning: By adjusting the difficulty and pace of learning, LLMs can optimize the learning experience for each student.

Intelligent Tutoring Systems: LLMs can provide real-time feedback and support, acting as virtual tutors.

Enhanced Student Engagement

Interactive Learning Experiences: LLMs can create engaging and interactive learning experiences, such as simulations, games, and role-playing scenarios.

Creative Writing and Problem-Solving: LLMs can assist students in developing their creative writing skills and problem-solving abilities.

Language Learning: LLMs can provide language practice, translation, and cultural insights.

Teacher Support

Automated Administrative Tasks: LLMs can automate tasks like grading, providing feedback, and generating lesson plans, freeing up teachers' time.

Professional Development: LLMs can offer personalized professional development opportunities, such as suggesting relevant articles, courses, or workshops.

Curriculum Development: LLMs can assist in creating engaging and effective curriculum materials.

Challenges and Considerations

While LLMs offer immense potential, it's important to address potential challenges and ethical considerations:

Bias and Fairness: LLMs can perpetuate biases present in their training data, leading to unfair outcomes.

Misinformation: LLMs can generate misleading or false information if not carefully trained and monitored.

Dependency: Overreliance on LLMs can reduce critical thinking and problem-solving skills.

To maximize the benefits of LLMs in education, it's essential to use them as tools to enhance learning, rather than as replacements for human interaction. By carefully considering their limitations and potential biases, we can harness the power of LLMs to create a more equitable and effective education system.

5.3 LLMs in Creative Writing and Content Generation

Large Language Models (LLMs) have emerged as powerful tools for creative writing and content generation. Their ability to process and generate human-quality text has opened up new possibilities for writers, marketers, and content creators.

Creative Writing Applications

Storytelling: LLMs can generate creative stories, poems, and scripts.

Character Development: They can help develop complex and believable characters with unique backstories and personalities.

Dialogue Writing: LLMs can generate realistic and engaging dialogue for scripts and novels.

Style Imitation: They can mimic the writing style of specific authors or genres.

Content Generation

Article Writing: LLMs can generate news articles, blog posts, and product descriptions.

Social Media Content: They can create engaging social media posts, including captions and hashtags.

Email Marketing: LLMs can draft personalized email campaigns.

Marketing Copy: They can generate persuasive marketing copy, such as ad slogans and product descriptions.

Key Benefits of Using LLMs in Creative Writing and Content Generation:

Increased Productivity: LLMs can significantly speed up the content creation process.

Enhanced Creativity: They can inspire new ideas and creative approaches.

Improved Quality: LLMs can help ensure consistency and accuracy in content.

Scalability: They can generate large volumes of content quickly and efficiently.

Challenges and Considerations

Originality: LLMs can sometimes produce repetitive or generic content.

Factual Accuracy: Ensuring the accuracy of generated content, especially for factual topics.

Ethical Implications: Addressing potential biases and ensuring ethical use of LLMs.

Future Directions

As LLM technology continues to advance, we can expect even more innovative applications in creative writing and content generation. Some potential future developments include:

Hyper-realistic Text Generation: Creating text that is indistinguishable from human-written content

Interactive Storytelling: Developing interactive stories where readers can influence the narrative.

AI-Powered Writing Assistants: Providing real-time feedback, suggestions, and editing assistance.

By understanding the capabilities and limitations of LLMs, we can harness their power to enhance creativity and streamline content production.

Chapter 6

Ethical Considerations and Bias in LLMs

6.1 Bias in Training Data: A Significant Challenge for LLMs

A major challenge in developing and deploying LLMs is the potential for bias in the training data. This bias can be reflected in the model's outputs, leading to unfair and discriminatory outcomes.

Sources of Bias in Training Data:

Sampling Bias: When the training data is not representative of the real-world population, it can lead to biased models.

Labeling Bias: Errors or inconsistencies in labeling the training data can introduce bias into the model.

Algorithmic Bias: The algorithms used to train and deploy LLMs can inadvertently amplify biases present in the data.

Societal Bias: Training data often reflects societal biases and stereotypes, which can be perpetuated by the model.

Impact of Bias in LLMs:

Unfair Decisions: Biased LLMs can make unfair decisions, such as denying loans or job opportunities.

Stereotyping: LLMs can perpetuate harmful stereotypes about certain groups of people.

Misinformation: Biased models can generate misleading or false information.

Mitigating Bias in LLMs:

Diverse and Representative Data: Using diverse and representative training data can help reduce bias.

Fairness Metrics: Developing and using fairness metrics to evaluate the model's performance on different demographic groups.

Debiasing Techniques: Employing techniques like fair representation learning and adversarial debiasing to mitigate bias.

Human Oversight: Human oversight is essential to identify and correct biases in the model's outputs.

Transparency and Accountability: Being transparent about the model's limitations and potential biases.

By addressing these challenges and implementing effective mitigation strategies, we can develop LLMs that are fair, unbiased, and beneficial to society.

6.2 Ethical Implications of LLM Usage

The rapid advancement of Large Language Models (LLMs) has brought forth a host of ethical concerns that need careful consideration. Here are some of the key ethical implications:

1. Bias and Discrimination

Perpetuating Bias: LLMs can perpetuate biases present in their training data, leading to discriminatory outputs.

Fairness and Equity: Ensuring that LLMs are trained on diverse and unbiased data is crucial to avoid discriminatory outcomes.

2. Misinformation and Disinformation

Generating Misinformation: LLMs can generate misleading or false information, especially when prompted with biased or inaccurate queries.

Deepfakes and Synthetic Media: LLMs can be used to create deepfakes, which can be used to spread misinformation and deceive people.

3. Job Displacement and Economic Impact

Automation of Tasks: LLMs can automate tasks traditionally performed by humans, leading to job displacement.

Economic Inequality: The development and deployment of LLMs can exacerbate existing economic inequalities.

4. Privacy Concerns

Data Privacy: LLMs require large amounts of data, raising concerns about data privacy and security.

Surveillance and Monitoring: LLMs can be used to monitor and track individuals' online behavior.

5. Intellectual Property and Copyright

Ownership of Generated Content: Determining ownership rights over content generated by LLMs can be complex.

Copyright Infringement: LLMs may inadvertently generate content that infringes on existing copyrights.

Mitigating Ethical Risks

To address these ethical challenges, it is crucial to:

Develop Ethical Guidelines: Establish clear ethical guidelines for the development and deployment of LLMs.

Promote Transparency: Be transparent about the limitations and biases of LLMs.

Foster Responsible AI Development: Encourage responsible AI development practices, including rigorous testing and evaluation.

Educate the Public: Raise awareness about the potential risks and benefits of LLMs.

Collaborate with Policymakers: Work with policymakers to develop regulations and standards for AI.

By proactively addressing these ethical implications, we can harness the power of LLMs while minimizing their potential negative impacts.

6.3 Mitigating Bias and Ensuring Fairness in LLMs

Addressing bias in LLMs is a crucial task to ensure their ethical and responsible use. Here are some strategies to mitigate bias and promote fairness:

1. Diverse and Representative Training Data

Data Curation: Carefully curate training data to include diverse perspectives, backgrounds, and viewpoints.

Balanced Datasets: Ensure that the dataset is balanced across different demographic groups to avoid biases.

2. Fairness Metrics and Evaluation

Bias Detection Tools: Use tools to identify and measure bias in the model's outputs.

Fairness Metrics: Employ fairness metrics like demographic parity and equalized odds to evaluate the model's performance across different groups.

3. Debiasing Techniques

Fairness Constraints: Incorporate fairness constraints into the training process to penalize biased outputs.

Adversarial Debiasing: Train a separate model to identify and mitigate biases in the main model's outputs.

Data Augmentation: Augment the training data with diverse examples to reduce bias.

4. Human Oversight and Feedback

Human Review: Regularly review and correct biased or harmful outputs generated by the model.

User Feedback: Collect user feedback to identify and address biases.

5. Transparency and Explainability

Model Interpretability: Develop techniques to understand how the model makes decisions and identify potential biases.

Transparent Training Processes: Document the training process and data sources to increase accountability.

6. Continuous Monitoring and Improvement

Regular Evaluation: Continuously monitor the model's performance and identify emerging biases.

Iterative Refinement: Update and retrain the model to address identified biases and improve its performance.

By implementing these strategies, we can work towards developing LLMs that are fair, unbiased, and beneficial to society. It's important to note that mitigating bias is an ongoing process, and it requires a multi-faceted approach involving technical, ethical, and societal considerations.

Chapter 7

Building with LLMs: A Practical Guide

7.1 API Access to LLMs: A Gateway to AI Power

Large Language Models (LLMs) have revolutionized the field of AI, and accessing their capabilities through APIs has become increasingly popular. These APIs provide a convenient way to integrate LLM functionality into various applications, from chatbots and virtual assistants to content generation and code completion.

Popular LLM APIs

Here are some of the most popular LLM A

OpenAI API: Offers access to models like GPT-3.5 and GPT-4, known for their advanced language understanding and generation capabilities.

Can be used for a wide range of tasks, including text generation, summarization, translation, and code completion.

Google AI:

Provides access to Google's state-of-the-art language models, such as PaLM 2.

Offers APIs for various tasks, including text generation, translation, and question answering.

Hugging Face:

A platform for sharing and deploying machine learning models, including LLMs.

Offers access to a wide range of open-source LLMs, allowing developers to customize and fine-tune models for specific needs.

Cohere:

Provides a suite of language AI models, including language generation, summarization, and search.

Offers a user-friendly API for easy integration into applications.

How to Use LLM APIs

To use an LLM API, typically you'll follow these steps:

Sign Up: Create an account with the API provider.

Obtain an API Key: This key will be used to authenticate your requests and track usage.

Choose a Model: Select the LLM model that best suits your needs based on factors like performance, cost, and specific capabilities.

Make API Requests: Use the API provider's documentation to construct API requests, providing prompts or inputs to the model.

Process the Response: The API will return a response, often in JSON format, containing the generated text or other relevant information.

Key Considerations for Using LLM APIs

Cost: Many LLM APIs have usage-based pricing models, so it's important to consider the cost implications of your application.

Performance: The performance of an LLM can vary depending on the model and the specific task.

Latency: The latency of API requests can impact the user experience, especially for real-time applications.

Ethical Considerations: Be mindful of the ethical implications of using LLMs, such as bias and misinformation.

By effectively utilizing LLM APIs, developers can unlock the power of AI and create innovative applications that can transform various industries.

7.2 Prompt Engineering Techniques

Prompt engineering is the art of crafting effective prompts to guide LLMs towards generating desired outputs. By carefully constructing prompts, you can significantly improve the quality and relevance of the generated text. Here are some key techniques:

1. Clear and Specific Instructions

Directness: Provide clear and concise instructions.

Specificity: The more specific your prompt, the more accurate the output.

Example: Instead of "Write a poem," try "Write a sonnet about the beauty of nature, using vivid imagery and a melancholic tone."

2. Leverage the Power of Keywords

Keyword Guidance: Include relevant keywords to steer the model's focus.

Semantic Similarity: Use synonyms or related terms to broaden the scope of the generated text.

Example: To generate a summary of a scientific paper, provide keywords like "quantum computing," "superconductivity," and "quantum entanglement."

3. Utilize System Messages

Role-Playing: Define the role of the AI, such as a helpful assistant, a creative writer, or a technical expert.

Constraints and Guidelines: Set boundaries for the AI's responses, such as word count, style, or tone.

Example: "You are a knowledgeable AI assistant. Provide a concise summary of the key points in this article, avoiding technical jargon."

4. Iterative Refinement

Feedback Loops: Provide feedback on the initial output to guide the model towards the desired outcome.

Experimentation: Try different prompts and techniques to find the best approach.

Example: If the initial response is too formal, ask the model to be more casual and conversational.

5. Temperature Control

Creativity vs. Factuality: Adjust the temperature parameter to control the creativity and randomness of the generated text.

Higher Temperature: More creative and diverse outputs.

Lower Temperature: More focused and factual outputs.

6. Prompt Chaining

Sequential Prompts: Break down complex tasks into smaller, sequential prompts.

Building on Responses: Use the previous response as input for the next prompt.

Example: First, ask the model to write a short story. Then, provide the story as input and ask for a movie script adaptation.

By mastering these techniques, you can unlock the full potential of LLMs and generate high-quality, tailored content.

7.3 Fine-tuning LLMs for Specific Tasks

Fine-tuning is a technique that involves taking a pre-trained LLM and adapting it to a specific task or domain. By training the model on a relevant dataset, we can improve its performance and tailor it to our needs.

Key Techniques for Fine-tuning LLMs:

Supervised Fine-tuning:

Task-Specific Data: Collect or curate a dataset that is relevant to the target task.

Model Training: Train the pre-trained LLM on this dataset, adjusting its parameters to better fit the specific task.

Example: Fine-tuning a general-purpose LLM on a dataset of medical articles to create a medical question-answering system.

Prompt Engineering:

Crafting Effective Prompts: Carefully design prompts to elicit desired responses from the LLM.

Iterative Refinement: Continuously refine prompts based on the model's output to achieve better results.

Example: Using specific prompts to guide the LLM to write different creative text formats, such as poems, scripts, or code.

Parameter-Efficient Fine-tuning (PEFT):

Reducing Computational Cost: This technique involves fine-tuning only a small subset of the model's parameters, making it more efficient.

Preserving General Knowledge: By freezing most of the model's parameters, we can preserve its general knowledge while adapting it to specific tasks.

Example: Fine-tuning a large LLM on a smaller dataset to create a specialized chatbot.

Considerations for Fine-tuning LLMs:

Data Quality: Ensure the quality and relevance of the fine-tuning dataset.

Computational Resources: Fine-tuning LLMs can be computationally expensive, so consider using cloud-based solutions or specialized hardware.

Ethical Implications: Be mindful of potential biases in the training data and the ethical implications of the fine-tuned model's outputs.

Overfitting: Avoid overfitting by carefully tuning hyperparameters and using regularization techniques.

By effectively fine-tuning LLMs, we can unlock their full potential and create powerful AI applications tailored to specific needs.

Chapter 8

Future Trends and Innovations

8.1 Multimodal LLMs: The Future of AI

Multimodal LLMs are a cutting-edge development in the field of artificial intelligence, capable of processing and generating multiple modalities of data, such as text, images, and audio. These models are revolutionizing various industries by enabling more sophisticated and nuanced AI applications.

Key Capabilities of Multimodal LLMs:

Image and Text Understanding: Analyzing images and text together to extract deeper meaning and generate more relevant responses.

Text-to-Image Generation: Creating images based on textual descriptions.

Image-to-Text Generation: Generating descriptive text from images.

Audio and Text Understanding: Analyzing audio and text to extract information and generate responses.

Multimodal Generation: Creating various forms of content, such as text, images, and code, based on multimodal inputs.

Applications of Multimodal LLMs:

Enhanced Search Engines: Improving search results by considering both text and image queries.

Medical Image Analysis: Assisting doctors in diagnosing diseases by analyzing medical images

Content Creation: Generating creative content, such as stories, poems, and scripts, based on image or audio prompts.

Education: Creating personalized learning experiences by adapting to different learning styles and preferences.

Accessibility: Making information accessible to people with disabilities by providing alternative formats, such as text-to-speech and image descriptions.

Challenges and Future Directions

While multimodal LLMs hold immense potential, several challenges need to be addressed:

Data Quality and Quantity: High-quality, diverse, and aligned multimodal data is essential for training these models.

Computational Resources: Training and deploying multimodal LLMs requires significant computational resources.

Ethical Considerations: Addressing biases and ensuring fairness in multimodal AI is crucial.

The future of multimodal LLMs is promising, with potential applications in various fields. As technology continues to advance, we can expect to see even more sophisticated and powerful multimodal AI systems that can revolutionize the way we interact with the world.

8.2 Agent-Based LLMs: The Next Frontier

Agent-based LLMs represent a significant advancement in AI, allowing for more complex and autonomous behavior. These agents can plan, reason, and execute tasks in the real world or simulated environments.

Key Components of Agent-Based LLMs:

LLM Core: A powerful language model that serves as the "brain" of the agent.

Memory: A system to store and retrieve information, enabling the agent to learn from past experiences and adapt its behavior.

Planning: A module that allows the agent to break down complex tasks into smaller, actionable steps.

Action and Perception: The agent's ability to interact with the environment, whether it's a physical or digital space.

Potential Applications:

Customer Service: Agent-based LLMs can provide more personalized and efficient customer support, handling complex inquiries and resolving issues.

Education: Intelligent tutoring systems can be developed to provide tailored learning experiences for each student.

Healthcare: AI agents can assist in medical diagnosis, drug discovery, and patient care.

Creative Content Generation: Agents can generate creative content, such as articles, scripts, and code.

Robotics: Autonomous robots can be controlled by LLM agents to perform tasks in various environments.

Challenges and Future Directions:

While agent-based LLMs hold immense potential, several challenges need to be addressed:

Alignment: Ensuring that the agent's goals align with human values and avoid unintended consequences.

Safety: Developing safety mechanisms to prevent the agent from causing harm.

Scalability: Training and deploying large-scale agent-based systems.

Ethical Considerations: Addressing ethical implications, such as privacy and fairness.

The future of agent-based LLMs is promising, with the potential to revolutionize various industries. By addressing the challenges and exploring new frontiers, we can unlock the full potential of these advanced AI systems.

8.3 The Impact of LLMs on Society

Large Language Models (LLMs) are poised to significantly reshape society. Their potential benefits are vast, but so are the challenges and ethical considerations.

Potential Benefits

Increased Efficiency and Productivity: LLMs can automate tasks, freeing up human time for more creative and strategic work.

Improved Access to Information: LLMs can break down language barriers and provide access to information in various languages.

Enhanced Creativity: LLMs can assist in creative processes, such as writing, music composition, and design.

Advanced Healthcare: LLMs can analyze medical data to improve diagnosis and treatment.

Personalized Education: LLMs can tailor educational experiences to individual needs and learning styles.

Potential Challenges and Risks

Job Displacement: As LLMs become more advanced, they may replace human workers in certain industries.

Misinformation and Disinformation: Malicious actors can use LLMs to generate false or misleading information.

Bias and Discrimination: If LLMs are trained on biased data, they can perpetuate harmful stereotypes and discrimination.

Privacy Concerns: The use of LLMs raises concerns about data privacy and security.

Ethical Considerations: The development and deployment of LLMs must be guided by ethical principles to avoid unintended consequences.

Mitigating Risks and Maximizing Benefits

To fully realize the potential of LLMs while minimizing risks, we need to:

Develop Ethical Guidelines: Establish clear ethical guidelines for the development and deployment of LLMs.

Promote Transparency: Be transparent about the limitations and biases of LLMs.

Foster Responsible AI Development: Encourage responsible AI development practices, including rigorous testing and evaluation.

Educate the Public: Raise awareness about the potential risks and benefits of LLMs.

Collaborate with Policymakers: Work with policymakers to develop regulations and standards for AI.

By addressing these challenges and embracing ethical considerations, we can harness the power of LLMs to create a better future for all.

Chapter 9

Case Studies and Real-world Examples

9.1 Successful LLM Applications

Large Language Models (LLMs) have been successfully applied to a wide range of fields. Here are some notable examples:

1. Healthcare

Medical Diagnosis: LLMs can analyze medical records and symptoms to assist in diagnosis.

Drug Discovery: LLMs can accelerate drug discovery by analyzing vast amounts of biomedical literature.

Patient Care: LLMs can provide personalized medical advice and support.

2. Education

Personalized Learning: LLMs can tailor educational content to individual student needs.

Intelligent Tutoring Systems: LLMs can provide real-time feedback and guidance.

Language Learning: LLMs can facilitate language learning by providing personalized practice and feedback.

3. Customer Service

Chatbots: LLMs can power chatbots to provide 24/7 customer support.

Sentiment Analysis: LLMs can analyze customer feedback to identify trends and improve customer satisfaction.

Personalized Recommendations: LLMs can recommend products or services based on individual preferences.

4. Creative Writing

Content Generation: LLMs can generate articles, blog posts, and marketing copy.

Scriptwriting: LLMs can assist in scriptwriting by generating dialogue and plot ideas.

Poetry and Songwriting: LLMs can create poems and song lyrics.

5. Code Generation

Code Completion: LLMs can suggest code completions and generate code snippets.

Code Debugging: LLMs can identify and fix errors in code.

Code Documentation: LLMs can generate documentation for code.

6. Scientific Research

Literature Review: LLMs can quickly analyze and summarize scientific literature.

Hypothesis Generation: LLMs can generate new hypotheses based on existing knowledge.

Data Analysis: LLMs can analyze large datasets to identify patterns and trends.

As LLM technology continues to advance, we can expect to see even more innovative and impactful applications in the years to come.

9.2 Lessons Learned from LLM Failures

While LLMs have demonstrated remarkable capabilities, they are not without their limitations and pitfalls. Here are some key lessons learned from LLM failures:

1. Hallucinations and Factual Inaccuracies

Data Quality: The quality of training data significantly impacts the accuracy of LLM outputs.

Prompt Engineering: Carefully crafting prompts can reduce hallucinations and improve factual accuracy.

Fact-Checking and Verification: Implement mechanisms to verify the information generated by LLMs, especially when dealing with critical information.

2. Bias and Fairness

Diverse and Representative Data: Ensure that training data is diverse and representative to mitigate bias.

Regular Bias Auditing: Continuously monitor and address bias in the model's outputs.

Fairness Metrics: Utilize fairness metrics to evaluate the model's performance across different demographic groups.

3. Sensitivity to Prompting

Prompt Engineering Best Practices: Follow guidelines for effective prompt engineering to elicit desired responses.

Iterative Refinement: Experiment with different prompts and refine them based on the model's output.

Avoid Ambiguous Prompts: Be clear and specific in your prompts to minimize misunderstandings.

4. Computational Cost and Efficiency

Efficient Model Architectures: Explore efficient architectures like transformers with reduced complexity.

Hardware Optimization: Utilize specialized hardware like GPUs and TPUs to accelerate training and inference.

Quantization and Pruning: Employ techniques to reduce model size and computational cost.

5. Ethical Considerations

Responsible AI Development: Adhere to ethical guidelines and principles for AI development.

Transparency and Explainability: Make the model's decision-making process transparent and explainable.

User Safety: Implement safeguards to prevent malicious use of LLMs.

By learning from these lessons, we can develop more robust and reliable LLM applications that benefit society.

9.3 Future Possibilities of LLMs

The future of LLMs is incredibly promising, with the potential to revolutionize numerous industries and aspects of daily life. Here are some exciting possibilities:

1. Advanced AI Assistants

Personalized Assistants: LLMs can become highly personalized assistants, understanding individual preferences and tailoring responses accordingly.

Creative Collaboration: LLMs can collaborate with humans on creative projects, such as writing, music composition, and design.

2. Enhanced Education

Personalized Learning: LLMs can create customized learning experiences for each student.

Intelligent Tutoring Systems: LLMs can provide real-time feedback and support to students.

Language Learning: LLMs can facilitate language learning by providing personalized practice and feedback.

3. Healthcare Revolution

Drug Discovery: LLMs can accelerate drug discovery by analyzing vast amounts of biomedical data.

Medical Diagnosis: LLMs can assist in diagnosing diseases by analyzing medical images and patient records.

Personalized Medicine: LLMs can help develop personalized treatment plans for patients.

4. Sustainable Future

Climate Modeling: LLMs can analyze climate data to predict future trends and inform policy decisions.

Sustainable Agriculture: LLMs can optimize agricultural practices to reduce environmental impact.

Renewable Energy: LLMs can contribute to the development of renewable energy technologies.

5. Ethical AI

Bias Mitigation: LLMs can be developed with fairness and inclusivity in mind.

Transparency and Explainability: LLMs can be made more transparent, allowing users to understand their decision-making processes.

Responsible AI: LLMs can be used to promote ethical and responsible AI development.

To fully realize the potential of LLMs, it is crucial to address the challenges and ethical implications associated with their development and deployment. By working together, researchers, developers, and policymakers can ensure that LLMs are used for the betterment of society.

Chapter 10

Conclusion

10.1 Recap of Key Concepts

Large Language Models (LLMs) are a type of artificial intelligence that can understand and generate human language. They are trained on massive amounts of text data and can perform a variety of tasks, such as:

Text Generation: Creating articles, poems, scripts, or code.

Text Summarization: Condensing long texts into shorter summaries.

Machine Translation: Translating text from one language to another.

Question Answering: Answering questions based on a given[1] text

Sentiment Analysis: Identifying the sentiment expressed in a text.

Key Concepts Related to LLMs:

Neural Networks: The underlying architecture that powers LLMs.

Transformer Architecture: A specific neural network architecture that has revolutionized natural language processing.

Training Data: The data used to train LLMs.

Fine-tuning: The process of adapting a pre-trained LLM to a specific task.

Prompt Engineering: The art of crafting effective prompts to guide LLM outputs.

Bias and Fairness: The ethical implications of LLMs and the importance of mitigating bias.

Multimodal LLMs: LLMs that can process and generate multiple modalities of data, such as text, images, and audio.

Agent-Based LLMs: LLMs that can act autonomously in the real world or simulated environments.

Challenges and Future Directions

While LLMs have tremendous potential, there are challenges to address:

Bias and Fairness: Ensuring that LLMs are unbiased and fair.

Misinformation: Preventing LLMs from generating false or misleading information.

Ethical Implications: Considering the ethical implications of LLM development and deployment.

Computational Cost: Training and running large LLMs can be computationally expensive.

Despite these challenges, the future of LLMs is promising. As technology continues to advance, we can expect to see even more innovative and powerful LLM applications.

10.2 The Future of LLMs

The future of LLMs is incredibly promising, with the potential to revolutionize numerous industries and aspects of daily life. Here are some key trends and possibilities:

1. Enhanced Capabilities:

Multimodal Learning: LLMs will be able to process and generate multiple modalities of data, such as text, images, and audio, leading to more sophisticated and creative applications.

Improved Reasoning and Problem-Solving: LLMs will become better at reasoning, planning, and problem-solving, enabling them to tackle more complex tasks.

Enhanced Creativity: LLMs will be able to generate more creative and original content, such as music, poetry, and code.

2. Specialized LLMs:

Domain-Specific Models: LLMs will be tailored to specific domains, such as healthcare, finance, and law, leading to more accurate and reliable results.

Smaller, More Efficient Models: Smaller, more efficient LLMs will be developed to run on edge devices and reduce computational costs.

3. Ethical AI:

Bias Mitigation: Efforts will be made to address bias in LLMs and ensure fair and equitable outcomes.

Transparency and Explainability: LLMs will be designed to be more transparent, making their decision-making processes easier to understand.

Responsible AI: The development and deployment of LLMs will be guided by ethical principles to minimize potential harm.

4. Human-AI Collaboration:

Augmented Intelligence: LLMs will augment human capabilities, allowing us to work more efficiently and creatively.

Collaborative Problem-Solving: LLMs will work alongside humans to solve complex problems.

5. Real-World Applications:

Healthcare: LLMs will be used to analyze medical data, accelerate drug discovery, and improve patient care.

Education: LLMs will personalize learning experiences and provide intelligent tutoring.

Customer Service: LLMs will power advanced chatbots and virtual assistants, providing 24/7 support.

Creative Industries: LLMs will be used to generate creative content, such as music, art, and literature.

As LLM technology continues to evolve, we can expect to see even more innovative and impactful applications. By addressing the challenges and ethical considerations, we can harness the power of LLMs to create a better future for all.

10.3 The Role of LLMs in Shaping the Future

Large Language Models (LLMs) are poised to significantly shape the future, impacting various aspects of our lives.[1]Here's a breakdown of their potential roles:

Revolutionizing Industries:

Healthcare:

Assisting in medical research and drug discovery

Providing personalized medical advice

Analyzing medical images for early disease detection

Education:

Personalizing learning experiences for students

Automating administrative tasks for teachers

Creating engaging educational content

Customer Service:

Powering advanced chatbots and virtual assistants

Analyzing customer feedback to improve products and services

Providing personalized customer support

Creative Industries:

Generating creative content like articles, scripts, and code

Assisting in design and art

Composing music and writing poetry

Transforming Human-Computer Interaction:

Natural Language Interfaces: Enabling more natural and intuitive interactions with computers

Intelligent Assistants: Providing personalized assistance in various tasks

Enhanced Accessibility: Making technology more accessible to people with disabilities

Ethical Considerations and Future Challenges:

While the potential of LLMs is immense, it's crucial to address ethical concerns:

Bias and Fairness: Ensuring that LLMs are trained on diverse and unbiased data to avoid perpetuating harmful stereotypes.

Misinformation: Mitigating the risk of LLMs generating false or misleading information.

Job Displacement: Addressing the potential impact of LLMs on employment.

Privacy and Security: Protecting user privacy and data security.

As LLM technology continues to advance, it's essential to strike a balance between innovation and ethical considerations. By addressing these challenges and embracing responsible AI development, we can harness the power of LLMs to create a better future for all.